Superstitions, Folklore, Myths & Legends

The Origins, History & Facts of Popular Wives' Tales

Scott Matthews

Copyright © 2022 Scott Matthews

All rights reserved. No part of this publication may be reproduced, distributed or transmitted in any form or by any means, including photocopying, recording, or other electronic or mechanical methods, without the prior written permission of the publisher, except in the case of brief quotations embodied in critical reviews and certain other non-commercial uses permitted by copyright law.

Trademarked names appear throughout this book. Rather than use a trademark symbol with every occurrence of a trademarked name, names are used in an editorial fashion, with no intention of infringement of the respective owner's trademark. The information in this book is distributed on an "as is" basis, without warranty. Although every precaution has been taken in the preparation of this work, neither the author nor the publisher shall have any liability to any person or entity with respect to any loss or damage caused or alleged to be caused directly or indirectly by the information contained in this book.

"The more that you read, the more things you will know. The more you learn, the more places you'll go."

- Dr. Seuss

ABOUT THE AUTHOR

Scott Matthews is a geologist, world traveller and author of the "Amazing World Facts" series! He was born in Brooklyn, New York, by immigrant parents from Ukraine but grew up in North Carolina. Scott studied at Duke University where he graduated with a degree in Geology and History.

His studies allowed him to travel the globe where he saw and learned amazing trivial knowledge with his many encounters. With the vast amount of interesting information he accumulated, he created his best selling books "Random, Interesting & Fun Facts You Need To Know."

He hopes this book will provide you with hours of fun, knowledge, entertainment and laughter.

BONUS!

Thanks for supporting me and purchasing this book! I'd like to send you some freebies. They include:

- The digital version of *500 World War I & II Facts*
- The digital version of *101 Idioms and Phrases*
- The audiobook for my best seller *1144 Random Facts*

Go to the last page of the book and scan the QR code. Enter your email and I'll send you all the files. Happy reading!

Contents

1. Horseshoes 1
2. Four-leaf clover 2
3. Crossing your fingers 3
4. Stars & astrology 4
5. Never speak when a clock is chiming 5
6. Never open an umbrella indoors 6
7. Bad things happen in threes 7
8. Tasseomancy 8
9. Bermuda triangle 10
10. Never kill a swallow 11
11. Never leave a rocking chair rocking when empty 12
12. If a picture falls off the wall, the person depicted will die soon 13
13. Friday the 13th 14
14. Never cut an elder tree 15
15. Werewolves 16
16. The gift of a purse or wallet should always include money 17
17. Yule logs prevent lightning from striking 18
18. Babies 19
19. Spitting to ward off evil 20
20. Never kill a spider 21
21. Carrying a rabbit's foot to ward off evil 22
22. Dreams 23
23. Putting salt on the doorstep of a new house to ward off evil 24
24. It's unlucky to kill an albatross 25
25. Funerals 26
26. Human bones 28
27. Evil spirits cannot harm a person standing inside a circle 29
28. When a dog howls, death is near 30
29. Unicorns 31
30. Itching palms 32
31. St. Johns wort guards against the devil 33
32. Walking underneath a ladder 34
33. It's bad luck to pass anyone on the staircase 35
34. Numbers 36
35. A loaf of bread turned upside down after slicing is perilous 38
36. Left-handed people 39
37. Ouija boards 40
38. It's bad luck to let milk boil over 42
39. Placing shoes upon a table will bring bad luck 43
40. Covering the mouth when yawning 44
41. Never take a broom with you when you move house 45
42. Never use a crossroads as a meeting place 46
43. Palmistry 47
44. Pirates 48

45. Vampires	50
46. Never speak ill of the dead	51
47. Spicy food causes ulcers	52
48. Scissors	53
49. Never kill a robin	54
50. Saying bless you when someone sneezes	55
51. The evil eye	56
52. Never bring lilies indoors	57
53. Wishbones	58
54. Black cats	59
55. Ravens	60
56. The black death	61
57. Candles	62
58. Owls	63
59. Bigfoot	64
60. Burning cheeks mean someone is talking about you	66
61. Picking up pennies	67
62. Keeping cats away from babies	68
63. Ships as "she"	69
64. The first person you see on new year's day must be a dark haired man	70
65. Knock on wood	71
66. Seeing a shooting star	72
67. Spilling salt	73
68. Carrying a toadstone to protect against evil and cure illness	74
69. Tying a knot in a handkerchief	75
70. Gravestones	76
71. Crossed knives at the table signify a quarrel	77
72. Always stir christmas pudding clockwise	78
73. Frogs	79
74. Covering mirrors after a death in the home	80
75. Magpies	81
76. Full moon	82
77. Bats want to nest in women's hair	84
78. Loose or broken shoelaces	85
79. Bringing a hawthorn branch into the house will bring death	86
80. Holding your breath when passing a cemetery	87
81. Acorns protect your house from lightning	88
82. Breaking a mirror	89
83. Pregnancy	90
84. Nessie	92
85. Voodoo dolls	93
86. Never light three cigarettes with one match	94
87. Water	95
88. Lady luck	96
Bonus	97

Introduction

Have you ever had a feeling that you couldn't explain? Has your stomach ever had butterflies or your skin tingled, and you wonder why? Have you looked up into the starry night and wondered what is beyond? Do your dreams ever come true? What if the answers to our hopes and the quelling of our fears is as close as a flick of salt, a knock on wood, a crack of a wishbone, or a crossing of fingers?

Humankind has always searched for explanations of the impossible, meaning in the mundane, and assurance during uncertain times. It is our desire for understanding and security that has led to the establishment of superstitions, traditions, and folklore.

We are constantly trying to make sense of the natural world and often ascribe supernatural forces to the elements of reality that aren't easily explained. Oftentimes, these beliefs are codified into organized religions that establish a firm ground for people to stand upon. Sometimes, the things we believe stay as rumors and tales, kept fresh by word of mouth through generations and maintained by the subtly of our subconscious which keeps us looking for patterns in our chaotic existence.

The word superstition is derived from the Latin words super (beyond or above) and stare (to stand). A rough translation might be "standing over," but not in the physical sense. The use of this word has evolved from the Greeks to the Romans to modern times. There is a sense that the prefix *super* links the fact that superstitions were deemed above and beyond the normal activities of everyday life and the standard religious and cultural practices.

There is another interpretation of the ancient word superstare: "to survive." Superstitions, despite murky origins and dubious reliability, are essentially survival memes. Most superstitions are passed on from one person or culture to another, morphing to fit into the contemporary belief system. This isn't done consciously, if the superstitions have merit to a particular group or region of the world then they will survive in the minds of the people.

Superstitions and old wives' tales are often imperative and dramatic.

Whether it concerns the health of a child, the salvation of a soul, the protection against death, the discovery of a secret, or the love of a partner; superstitions claim to have avenues for all manner of vital life events. Perhaps that is why superstitions can survive for decades, centuries, or millennia—they claim to protect against the worst of fates and grant the greatest joys of life.

Some superstitions started from mythologies of Greek heroes or Egyptian gods, only to be adapted by new religions or cultures. Other superstitions are in their infancy, having just been conceived within the last hundred years. There is no rule or regiment to establish a new superstition. The only requirement is that it is attractive in people's minds; once enough individuals latch onto it then it evolves and spreads on its own. To stop a superstition would be impossible on the level of one person, these ideas take on a life of their own, and what one person might deem far-fetched another could see as comforting.

When we think of a superstition, we liken it to an irrational belief. This belief might have a process or ritual that follows, often meant to prevent or attract an outcome. A rational person might ask: how can saying "bless you" or covering your mouth while yawning truly offer protection from supernatural forces? Is there any proof that these habits and rituals are effective?

This might be the wrong way to look at superstitions. Instead, consider the comfort and confidence one might earn by doing a superstitious act in the precise way you were taught by your elders. When important tasks need to be done and big decisions must be made, we want to know that others who came before had a method for achieving a goal or avoiding a terrible fate.

Sailors, doctors, priests, midwives, soldiers, tailors, farmers—they can all have specific rituals that help them do their job. If it worked for them, it should work for you. After all, our family, community, and culture raise us and teach us the skills we need to survive and the values that we hold dear. Why should a small gesture, like avoiding going under a ladder or stirring pudding in a certain direction, have any less adherence than the other lessons we are taught in life?

Many superstitions are a result of a shared heritage and culture. This shared experience could be from a religious group, ethnic group, country, profession, or community. A superstition is similar in many ways to a story. This story is one that everyone in the community knows by heart; they can repeat the story word for word, follow its directions, understand its consequences, and be assured by its prevalence and longevity that this story is important to pass along to others. Who's to say what is fact and what is superstition?

1. Horseshoes

A horseshoe sounds like a random object to be linked to good luck, and there isn't a clear historical reason as to why. Perhaps because horseshoes are an extremely practical invention and they are shaped like a crescent moon. The most influential tale about horseshoes is from a Christian tale about St. Dunstan nailing the Devil to a wall while painfully shoeing his hoofed feet with horseshoes. He made the Devil promise to never enter a home with a horseshoe hung above the doorway. Since that tale, superstitious folk have nailed horseshoes (often with seven nails) above their doorways. This could be done upside down or U-shaped as some people have different interpretations as to which way secures luck and safety. In the Middle Ages, when fears of witches ran rampant, many households would nail horseshoes to their doors, as it was rumored that witches couldn't cross the threshold under a horseshoe. Nowadays, jewelry is sold in the shape of a horseshoe and some brides-to-be might carry a cloth horseshoe on their wedding day to ensure a good marriage. Another superstition says that if you sleep with a horseshoe under your pillow on New Year's Eve, the new year will be full of prosperity for you.

2. Four-leaf clover

The four-leaf clover is one of the most well-known symbols of luck. Nowadays, we can see this universal symbol for good luck almost everywhere—logos of different brands, markings, prints, and Internet emojis. But what is the basis for this tiny plant being related to luck? One reason the four-leaf variety of clover is prized is its rarity. It is estimated that 1-100 in 10,000 specimens have four leaves. However, the four-leaf clover can easily be mixed up with Oxalis deppei, a different plant that always has four leaves and looks a lot like the famous amulet. In Celtic folklore, the four-leaf clover was believed to enhance one's connection to the spiritual world. It was believed that these talismans could help a person see fairies and sense evil spirits coming. It was common practice for Druids (Celtic priests) to carry four-leaf clovers. As Christianity spread, it became a symbol for St. Patrick, the Saint Protector of Ireland. One Irish belief is that the first three leaves of the clover represent faith, hope, and love, while the fourth leaf stands for God's grace, a different term for luck. There also exists a Christian legend that says when Adam and Eve were leaving the Garden of Eden, Eve took a four-leafed clover to remember her days in the Garden. And, for the rest of their earthly lives, the plant from paradise gave them luck.

3. CROSSING YOUR FINGERS

Have you ever crossed your fingers in the hope that your wish might come true? You are not alone. For thousands of years "fingers crossed" has been synonymous with good luck. It may pre-date Christianity, but one of the first widespread uses of crossing fingers was among early Christians who had to hide their faith. Two Christians might meet and cross fingers with each other in order to affirm their "secret" that they were both Christians. While crossed fingers don't look like a literal cross, the symbolism stuck around throughout history. This evolved over the centuries to a person by themselves crossing their fingers in order to protect themselves from a bad omen or to ensure that a positive outcome would occur. Soldiers in the Hundred Years War between England and France even crossed their fingers before going into battle. But why do kids cross their fingers behind their backs when they are telling a lie? It might be because they are hoping to be "lucky" and not get caught in the lie.

4. Stars & Astrology

For millennia, humans have looked up into the sky and marveled. Nearly all civilizations in history have created some form of myths and legends based on the movement of the stars and the phenomena of the night sky. Ancient Persians believed that some constellations were guardians of the sky. The Greeks used the stars in much of their folklore, including the story of the Titan Atlas, who was tasked by Zeus to carry the heavens on his shoulders. One of the most famous constellations, Orion's Belt, comes from the Greek myth of the Boeotian giant Orion who pursued the Pleiades (Orion's daughters) across the night sky. Across Africa, too, ancient cultures derived their myths from the stars. The Tswana ethnic group thought that the stars were the souls of those unwilling to be born. The Venda, a South African Bantu people, believed that the stars were hanging by cords from the solid dome of the sky. Have you ever seen a shooting star? In the present day, some superstitious folk might wish upon a shooting star or say "money" three times in order to gain wealth. Astrology and Tarot cards are another form of interpreting the positions of stars in the cosmos that many people use today to predict fortunes or relationships.

5. Never speak when a clock is chiming

Before cell phones, batteries, and electricity, clocks kept time mechanically and had to be winded up in order to work. A wound clock wouldn't keep time forever; but sometimes, even after stopping its "tick-tock," the clock would spring to life suddenly and chime, often scaring the wits out of the occupants of a home. These occurrences began to take on a superstition of their own and many believed that when a stopped clock chimed, then a death in the house would occur. The ominous nature of clocks persisted in the industrialized world. Another superstition demanded that no one speak during the chiming of a clock; it was considered bad luck and could spell misfortune for the one who dared to speak. In 1873, the Reverend Samuel Watson wrote an entire book detailing accounts of supernatural events including stopped clocks suddenly chiming followed by a death in the home. Nowadays, the omen of a chiming clock mostly lives on in horror movies. Somehow, the myth has morphed so that if you wake up suddenly at three in the morning, evil forces are afoot. Or, if a clock chimes mysteriously at three in the morning, then the person who awakens is about to die.

6. Never open an umbrella indoors

It sounds innocent: you open an umbrella inside a friend's house. But wait, they tell you that you might get bad luck "raining" down on you. Where does this superstition come from? As far back as ancient Egypt, people have used umbrellas. Around 1200 BCE, the Egyptians used umbrellas made of peacock feathers and papyrus (a material similar to thick paper that was used in ancient times as a writing surface) to shade themselves from the sun. Supposedly, opening an umbrella inside was bad luck in Egypt because opening it away from the sun's rays would displease the sun god, Ra. In the 1800s, when Samuel Fox invented the modern umbrella frame, it was spring-loaded and when opened could cause injury to nearby people. Just imagine opening a large, steel-ribbed umbrella indoors; objects could be broken and people sent ducking for cover. This modern superstition comes from a more practical place than most. A more wary person might also believe the myths that an umbrella should not be given as a gift and that if you drop your umbrella you should ask someone else to pick it up for you or you'll have bad luck.

7. Bad things happen in threes

Is the number three some sort of ominous, magical number? Probably not, but that hasn't stopped people's imaginations from running wild. The old phrases "accidents come in threes," "three's a crowd," or "death comes in threes" might simply stem from the fact that humans see patterns where they don't necessarily exist (called apophenia). The number three has some historical attributions (the Holy Trinity, a "family unit" of three, people often have three names in western civilization) but some old superstitions also state that three is unlucky. Three butterflies on one leaf, three hoots from an owl, and "three times a bridesmaid, never a bride" have been taken from western folklore as bad omens. More recently, people have looked at the deaths of celebrities as happening in groups of three. This superstition seems to be born out of old ideas about three being unlucky but, in reality, someone on Earth dies an average of .5 seconds every day, so simply hearing about three people out of the multitude of worldwide deaths is pure coincidence. It has become so common that the fear of the number three even has a name: triaphilia.

8. Tasseomancy

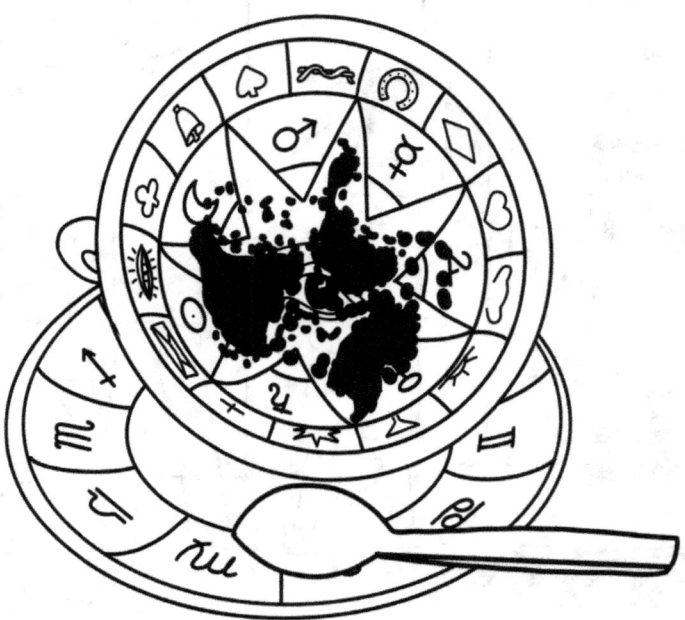

Pronounced "tass-ee-oh-man-see." The term derives from the French word 'tasse' (cup), which in turn derives from the Arabic word 'tassa,' and the Greek suffixe 'mancy' (divination).

Tasseomancy, also known as tasseography or tassology, is a method of fortune-telling that looks at the patterns in tea leaves, coffee grounds, or wine sediments. The shapes and patterns left behind in the cup can be interpreted to see into the past or predict the drinker's future.

The ancient Greeks had specific methods of reading the future, using wine instead of tea. They called this fortune-telling practice Kottovos and Greek seers would throw wine into a container and follow the shape that the splash would make. The sedimentation at the bottom of the cup would create an image that was used by the fortune-teller to interpret the future.

Coffee reading is traditionally done with Arabic or Turkish coffee because these types of coffee beans leave behind thick sedimentation. Some fortune-tellers split the coffee cup into two halves, where one half represents the past and the other the future. Others use the halves to answer specific questions with one half of the cup representing yes and the other no.

In western culture, the medieval fortune-tellers developed similar versions of divination as they would read patterns from wax, iron, lead, and other melted materials. The modern variant of tea leaf reading started in the seventeenth century when tea was imported from China to Europe. The practice strongly resembles the ancient Greek methods of looking at the leftover sediments at the bottom of the cup and interpreting the patterns.

Tasseomancy exists today alongside other superstitious practices like Tarot cards and seances that might fall under the umbrella of "fortune-tellers." The Roma people of Europe, often called gypsies, used fortune-telling as a way to earn money and gain access to the elites of society. The stereotypical fortune-teller that one might see in a circus is dressed like a nineteenth century gypsie. They might perform palm readings or tasseomancy to any gullible customers.

Over the years, many universal symbols were developed for tea and coffee reading:

A Snake represents enmity or falsehood;
An Angel which represents good news;
A Spade means good fortune in work;
A Crescent moon represents changes;
A Mountain represents a journey of hindrance;
A House which implies change and success;
A Circle means wedding or love;
A Cross means addition;
A Bird represents travel;
Waves represent unity;
A Star represents good luck;
A Spiral symbolizes creativity.

9. Bermuda Triangle

The Bermuda Triangle (also known as the "Devil's Triangle") is a section of the Atlantic Ocean ranging from Bermuda to Miami and down to Puerto Rico. This massive area of the sea is rumored to be cursed; with missing ships, communication blackouts, mysterious storms, and navigation problems with aircraft all being reported. However, the fear of this area has only been around since the second half of the twentieth century, showing that superstitions don't have to have ancient origins. Writer Edward Van Winkle Jones popularized the Bermuda Triangle in 1950 when he penned an article about Flight 19, a U.S. Navy training flight with fourteen crew members that flew into the Atlantic Ocean and never came back. Also, the search and rescue plan that went to look for the flight was also lost. Over the subsequent decades, the number of missing planes and ships began to pile up, with entire crews gone missing, often with no S.O.S. signals or shipwrecks found. The weather can be strong and erratic in this part of the ocean but it might be the human imagination that has caused so much fear around the Bermuda Triangle. Other parts of the world's oceans are just as deadly, but once a myth starts it can be hard to put doubts to rest.

10. Never kill a swallow

The swallow has been recognized as an omen for thousands of years. These agile birds aren't domesticated and can travel great distances, so to have a swallow's nest on your farm or property was considered good luck in Scottish and English folklore. Conversely, if the swallow died or suddenly abandoned its nest it could spell misfortune. Swallows were traditionally looked at as birds of "freedom" as they can travel hundreds of miles across land and sea. An old French superstition says that if a swallow lands on one's shoulder then death is lurking nearby. The swallow was sacred to Aphrodite, the Greek goddess of love and beauty. Swallows were said to contain the souls of the deceased. While birds like pheasants and chickens have been used as a food source for centuries, to kill a swallow was seen as a very bad omen in many western cultures as swallows were said to contain the souls of the deceased. A myth of dubious origin, though stated in ancient Greece and carried into the pagan cultures of Europe, states that swallows could carry two precious "stones" in their bodies, one red and one black, that had magical properties and could ward against evil.

11. Never leave a rocking chair rocking when empty

It sounds innocent enough to simply stand up from a rocking chair—but wait! There's an old wive's tale that says if an empty rocking chair keeps rocking then evil spirits will be welcomed to sit in the chair. This superstition may originate from Irish folklore centuries ago but it has been kept alive by the southern states in America, where rocking chairs and porches are a staple of southern living. Elders will scold young children if they walk by and rock an empty chair just for the sake of it. Of course, a breeze might catch a rocking chair and cause it to move a bit, startling any superstitious folk. The only remedy is to sit in the chair until it stops moving, then you can safely get up and go about your day.

12. If a picture falls off the wall, the person depicted will die soon

What if a picture frame falls off a wall, but no one touches it? One grim superstition states that the person depicted will soon die, especially if the glass in the frame breaks. Other versions of this folklore say that if the person in the picture is already dead, then the spirit of the deceased purposefully knocked their picture frame off the wall to let their family know that they are still around, watching them. Supposedly, if a picture of a couple crashes to the floor, then their days together are numbered. What about a group photo? If the glass cracks along a certain person's body in the picture then that could spell back luck for the individual. The origin of this superstition is unknown, it was around before glass was used in frames and is perhaps related to the general fear of spirits moving otherwise stationary objects in a house, commonly called a poltergeist in popular culture today.

13. Friday the 13th

Can an entire day be unlucky for everyone? The idea that bad luck can occur on any Friday that falls on the 13th of the month (this can happen up to three times a year) is one of the most well-known superstitions. The number thirteen is considered unlucky all on its own; in fact, there is a name for a fear of the number: triskaidekaphobia (triskaideka is greek for thirteen; pronounced "tris-kai-deck-uh-pho-bee-a"). There isn't a particular reason why Friday would be unlucky, although it might stem, in part, because it was supposedly the day that Jesus was crucified. In 1307 (on Friday the 13th of October) hundreds of Knights Templar were arrested by the King of France and many were later executed, but the legend didn't seem to gain traction until six hundred years later. The true beginning of the superstition most likely stems from a book by Thomas Lawson titled "Friday, the Thirteenth." In this novel, a stockbroker chooses this date to purposefully crash the stock market and make himself rich in the process. Younger people today might have their ears perk up at the mention of the horror movie "Friday the 13th" which played off the fears of the infamous day and date.

14. Never cut an elder tree

Elder trees are common in the northern hemisphere, with white flowers and dark berries that are excellent for making pies, jams, or wine. In European folklore, especially among the British Isles, there is a plethora of myths surrounding these beautiful trees. Where you plant an elder tree has significance; plant a tree near your house for protection and prosperity, beside a barn to keep your livestock safe, or by bakeries and other stores where food is produced. The odor of an elder tree is a natural fly repellent, perhaps this is why they were said to protect against the Devil and witches, even though witches supposedly made headdresses out of elder tree twigs. Hiding under the tree was also rumored to be safe during a lightning storm (please don't attempt this one). Most of these superstitions have been attributed to the uniqueness and usefulness of elder trees, hence why cutting them down is considered very bad luck. All of the benefits of the "magical" protection, the smell, and the berries would be lost if you cut down this special tree. If the wood was used to make furniture then you could be doomed to be haunted. Furthermore, the burning of elder wood was considered a terrible omen, most likely because the wood tends to "hiss" and spit when burned. Some people thought that this was the Devil spitting.

15. Werewolves

A full moon; a piercing howl; sharp claws and fangs—beware the werewolf! It might sound like make-believe, but fear of werewolves, or lycan as they might be called, has been in existence for millenia. One of the oldest known texts, the *Epic of Gilgamesh*, tells the tale of a male turned into a wolf. Greek mythology has a story of Zeus turning the sons of Lycaon into wolves and the Norse have a story of wolf pelts turning a father and son into frenzied werewolves. The popularity of man-into-wolf legends grew through the centuries as murderers and butchers often claimed to have committed gruesome acts while transformed. A full moon has always brought about superstitious thoughts and the idea that predators, like wolves, would be active during a full moon was understood to be common. Ideas about how to stop werewolves usually involved a medical or spiritual intervention in the past. The concepts of shooting them with silver arrows or bullets or that a bite from a werewolf causes another to turn into a werewolf on the next full moon are fabrications from recent times; most notably, the 1941 film "The Wolf Man" brought werewolves back into popular culture.

16. The gift of a purse or wallet should always include money

A new wallet or purse seems like a sensible gift for a loved one, but an old wive's tale cautions against giving one without any money inside. The goal is not to give a large sum to the person getting the gift, often the amount being gifted might only be a coin or a dollar, but rather to help the recipient gain good luck in the hopes that the small amount given will attract more money. A variant of this superstition says that one should never leave a purse or wallet empty. Also, in Chinese lore, putting a purse on the ground is considered a sign of disregard for one's own money and should be avoided (plus, someone could steal it). Some cultures preferred silver as a gift inside a wallet, as silver has historically been very valuable.

17. Yule logs prevent lightning from striking

In modern times, a "yule log" might just be a big log placed in a hearth on Christmas Eve. But that tradition has morphed over centuries. In Nordic countries hundreds of years ago, people would cut down whole trees and stick one end into the fire so that it would burn for many nights. This tradition shifted to smaller yule logs and, when Christmas became a common tradition, a superstition about keeping the yule log burning for the twelve days of Christmas was created. It was said that the remains of the log should be kept in the house until the following Christmas and that the burnt yule log would prevent lightning from striking the house. But remember, never throw out the ashes of a yule log on Christmas, it's considered bad luck!

18. Babies

Old wives' tales don't care if you are big or small, there's always precautions to take and rituals to practice. Taking care of babies and ensuring that they grow up healthy and strong is a full-time job, one that many cultures have added a bit of superstition alongside. In Russia, it is bad luck for a baby to have their picture taken before they are one month old, as someone might look at the newborn with the "evil eye." In Greece, many households try to avoid newborns from seeing their reflection in a mirror until they have their christening; stemming from an old belief that their soul will be taken if they do. In many Jewish families, there is no pre-birth celebration or setup for a new baby. They often avoid discussing possible names in public, don't have a baby shower, and don't build the nursery. This tradition is probably left over from the past when infant mortality used to be far more commonplace. In Japan, they have several milestones for a baby: the seventh night after being born the baby's name is officially announced, when they turn one month old they go for their first visit to a shrine, and when they celebrate their one year birthday it's considered a blessing if they can walk and carry mochi (a Japanese rice cake made of mochigome, a short-grain rice) on their back.

19. Spitting to Ward off Evil

In modern times, spitting is often seen as rude or unsanitary. But, throughout history, spitting was seen as a way to protect against disease, misfortune, and evil spirits. In the Gospel of John, there is an event when Jesus Christ spits, mixes the dirt from the ground with his saliva, and uses the mix to return sight to a blind man. The Roman historian Pliny the Elder wrote about the act of spitting among the ancient Romans. In his description, he says: "We are in the habit of spitting to avoid contagion." In ancient Greece, superstitious Greeks would spit when passing by people who were sick with epilepsy because the disease was believed to be caused by malevolent spirits. The superstition lives to this day in Greek culture, as Greek people are known to make spitting or 'ftou' sounds three times while flicking their hand towards a person. This custom is seen as a compliment because the one performing the act is conveying that this person is worthy of jealousy. Spitting as a symbol of good luck has translated into modern times. A common ritual among fishermen is spitting on the nets in order to invite luck when fishing. Many athletes spit on their baseball bats, gloves, sports shoes, and balls to improve their grip, invite good luck, or as a personal ritual that helps them focus.

20. Never kill a spider

Since the dawn of civilization, spiders have been omens in many cultures across the world. Generally, spiders have been seen as symbols of good fortune and have even played a part in the founding myths of major religions. In Christianity, when Mary, Joseph, and Jesus were pursued by King Herod's men, they hid in a cave. Spiders spun a web over the entrance, so when the king's men came to the cave, they assumed no one was inside because the spiders' webs were intact. In the Torah, a similar story is told about King David who hides in a cave from King Saul. There, too, spiders' webs protect the entrance. In Islam, the prophet Muhammad hides in a cave where a tree and spider web protect the prophet from those that seek to harm him. In the industrialized world, we might shoo away or kill a spider, but that was taboo for millenia. One way to keep food fresh in olden times was to keep spiders where the food was stored as they would kill flies that might otherwise infest the food. There is even a rhyme that goes: "If you want to live and thrive, let the spider run alive," which explicitly forbids the killing of a spider, as it would impair one's good fortune.

21. Carrying a rabbit's foot to ward off evil

Keeping a "lucky" rabbit's foot in your pocket, that's not weird, right? One of the most recognizable talismans for good luck, a rabbit's foot (a fake one nowadays) has murky origins in history. Rabbits have been associated with fertility in various cultures around the globe and the Celts thought the animals were symbols of luck as far back as 600 BCE. The modern inspiration is likely a combination of African American and European superstitions. The "hand of glory" was a gruesome, medieval European belief that the hand of a hanged man, cut off and pickled, was a lucky charm. When slaves were brought from Africa to the Americas, they brought their own spiritual beliefs about rabbits and fertility. Somewhere along the line, the idea that the left hindfoot of a rabbit was a lucky totem came about. Even further, the superstitious folk believed that the rabbit from which the foot comes should be killed in a cemetery, if possible at midnight and on a full moon. The idea is that sacrificing the animal in such a specific way will greatly increase the "magic" in the rabbit's foot. And, the meaner the person whose grave the rabbit is killed on, the stronger the luck of the rabbit's foot.

22. Dreams

Cultures across history have always looked to dreams as powerful omens. Some even believe that the position one sleeps or their sleeping arrangement can have a profound effect on their dreams. One superstition states that if you get interrupted while making your bed, then you will have bad dreams that night. Other odd interactions, like leaning a broom against the bed, leaving shoes underneath the bed, having a mirror facing the bed, or getting out of bed on the opposite side that you climbed in, can all lead to misfortune. Another superstition says that a woman who falls asleep with a piece of wedding cake under the pillow will see her future husband in her dreams. Subsequently, if that same woman marries the man of her dreams, then the first person who falls asleep on their wedding night will be the first to die. Changing the bedding on Friday is considered bad luck, but the superstition doesn't have a clear origin. Perhaps it stems from Christian tradition, where Jesus was crucified and Eve gave Adam the forbidden apple—both on Fridays.

23. Putting salt on the doorstep of a new house to ward off evil

Salt has been used throughout history by many pagan cultures to ward off evil spirits. Some say that sprinkling salt in the corners of a house will balance the "energy" of the house. An older tradition tells new, suspicious homeowners to place a line of salt over the entryway of a house. This is to ensure that no maligned spirits can cross into the home. Supposedly, this will keep witches from being able to cross the threshold, too. An extension of this is to put salt along every doorway in the house so that every room is equally protected. Supposedly, mixing other herbs (like rosemary, cinnamon, ginger) can increase the effectiveness of the salt line in combating evil forces.

24. It's unlucky to kill an albatross

Sailors can be a superstitious lot, as traveling the vast ocean can have untold perils and voyagers are often at the whims of nature. Killing a bird of the sea, like a seagull or albatross, is considered extremely unlucky. Most of this fear is exemplified in Samuel Taylor Coleridge's poem, *The Rime of the Ancient Mariner*. In the poem, when the wind dies down and the boat is stranded, the mariner blames an albatross and kills the bird. An albatross can fly hundreds of miles without landing, so sailors often perceived them to be supernatural animals. Sailors believed that the souls of past mariners rode with the albatross across the sea. Seeing an albatross is good luck because the spirit of a sailor is on the ocean with you; however, killing one is considered very bad luck indeed.

25. Funerals

How to deal with death, and a dead body, has always been a troubling conundrum for humans. It makes sense that the passing of a loved one would inspire superstitions and rituals. The biggest question of all might be "What happens after we die"?

This question enters the realm of conjecture, beliefs, and religion; but a practical issue still remains: "What do we do with the body of the recently deceased"?

The ancient Greeks put coins over the eyes of the dead and burned them in a funeral pyre. The coins were payment for the boatman, Charon, who ferried the souls of the dead across the River Styx and into the Underworld. The tradition continued for thousands of years, even Abraham Lincoln's eyes were covered by two silver half dollars.

At various times in history, the cultures of Hindus, Sikhs, Vikings, and Romans also cremated their dead. Many cultures have a funeral procession that might walk or drive from a funeral home to the cemetery or burial site.

Two things never to do when a funeral procession is coming: don't meet it head on and don't count the number of cars, both instances will bring you bad luck.

Pallbearers, those who carry the casket, are often required to wear gloves. This superstition took hold in popular culture during Victorian England. There was a fear of disease, so wearing gloves had some logic behind it, but for the most part people were worried about the spirit of the recently deceased person. It was believed that by holding the casket with a bare hand, you might be inviting the spirit into your own body, so wearing gloves was a form of protection.

26. Human bones

In civilized society, we don't spend too much time thinking about the bones of the dead. But, in many ancient cultures, the bones of a deceased person were thought to have magical powers or even retain some aspect of the person's soul. Disturbing someone's grave has been taboo for thousands of years and was often thought to curse the person who dared to defile the dead. Usually, it was either thieves trying to extract some valuables or jewelry, people looking for corpses for quasi-medical purposes, or practitioners of witchcraft or the magical arts who wanted the bones for their rituals. It is probably just made-up rumors that witches even existed, let alone used human bones to make potions or curse others. There are instances of fortune-telling practices from the ancient world using chicken bones or other animals as a way of telling the future, similar to tasseomancy or palm reading. However, human bones were sometimes viewed to have medicinal properties to early "doctors." Some folk-cures included mixing powdered bone with red wine to cure dysentery and using human skull shavings mixed with food or drink to cure epilepsy. Some Germanic and Scandinavian tribes would dry out the skulls of their enemies and use them as drinking vessels, supposedly to gain the strength of the man they killed.

27. Evil spirits cannot harm a person standing inside a circle

If you hear "magic" and "spells," you might scoff at such things as nothing more than superstitions and overactive imaginations. But many people, both past and present, have practiced various forms of "magic." Some practitioners in pagan cultures would draw a circle, often using chalk or directly into the dirt, to protect themselves against evil spirits or witches casting spells. In colonial America, even among the architecture of the Christian settlers, historians have found intertwined circles drawn on walls or cross beams as protection from evil. In Europe, these marks were called "apotropaic" marks and they were drawn often as flower patterns or overlapping circles. In more modern times, casting a "spell" or trying to align one's energy is often performed in a circle.

28. When a dog howls, death is near

Ever since the domestication of the dog 12,000-14,000 years ago, humans have created relationships—and superstitions—with man's best friend. In Norse mythology, Freyja (the goddess of death) rides a chariot pulled by cats; supposedly, the dogs on Earth will howl at its passing. In Celtic folklore, along with the foundations for Halloween, there is a superstition that dogs howl when a pack of phantom hounds are leading their master on a hunt for souls. Also, the Egyptian god Anubis was the deity of mummification and the afterlife and was depicted with a jackal's head. The Greeks, too, have the three-headed dog Cerberus as the guardian to the Underworld. Some people believe that dogs can "sense" things about the health and spirit of humans. An interesting superstition, which persists in the southern U.S. to this day, involves the howling of a dog. If a dog quickly howls twice at a man, or three times at a woman, then that person will soon die.

29. Unicorns

When most people think of unicorns, they picture a horse with a single horn on its head. But where did this mythical depiction come from? As far back as 400 BCE, a beast with a white body, purple head, and a multicolored horn was described in detail. Supposedly, Genghis Khan decided not to invade India after a unicorn bowed to him and, thinking it was the spirit of his dead father, he turned his army around. Medieval folklore gave the unicorn its most prevalent superstition: unicorns are drawn to young women who kept their honor and these women could control the creatures. Kings and Queens hoarded "unicorn horns" because they thought that they could cure poison. Perhaps the narwhal, a small whale from the Arctic Ocean with a long tooth that sticks out from its head, is the origin of unicorn myths. Queen Elizabeth I was given one such "horn" from an Arctic explorer and she had it placed among the Crown Jewels of England. Nowadays, unicorns are mostly left to our imagination and children's shows, but they still remain a symbol for virtue.

30. Itching palms

Everyone gets itchy sometimes, but what if your palm is randomly itchy and you don't know why? Some say that an itchy right palm means that money is coming your way while an itch in the left palm means that you will have to pay someone money. Oddly, the hands that do the giving and paying are reversed in some cultures. This myth was derived from western Europe and the Saxons, where they would rub their hands on silver to cure an ailment. This shifted to simply rubbing hands on silver to make more silver come their way and was later adopted by the Romans as well. A slightly different version tells us that rubbing an itchy palm on wood will bring someone good luck.

31. St. Johns Wort Guards Against the Devil

St. John's wort is a common shrub with yellow flowers. Once known as hypericum, it has been used for thousands of years as medicine or a spiritual talisman. As far back as ancient Greece, there are examples of the flowers hung over statues of gods to ward away evil spirits. This belief in the protection that the hypericum would confer persisted into pagan cultures across Europe. The people who celebrated summer solstice festivals, sometimes referred to as Midsummer's Eve, often threw the plant onto bonfires or wore them around their necks in order to protect against evil. The Catholic Church, in an effort to convert the pagans, co-opted the summer solstice celebrations by claiming that the festivals could still take place but that the fires were to be in commemoration of the birthday of John the Baptist. The bonfires still burned, this time in honor of a Christian saint. The hypericum burned along with it, giving rise to a new name: St. John's wort. Using the flowers to expel demons or the Devil out of a possessed person became common during the Middle Ages. In modern times, St. John's wort is taken as a natural antidepressant. Perhaps the old myths were onto something...

32. Walking underneath a ladder

Everyone knows to avoid walking underneath a ladder, but why? This superstition might have its roots 5,000 years ago in ancient Egypt. Egyptians viewed the triangle as a sacred symbol (hence the pyramids) and to pass under a ladder would disrupt the triangle that is formed by the ladder, wall, and floor. A similar folklore was picked up by followers of Christianity, as three is a holy number (the Father, Son, and Holy Spirit) so walking through the triangle formed by a leaning ladder is disrespectful to the Holy Trinity. Also, a ladder was leaning against the crucifix when Jesus was killed so that is more ammunition to contribute to the unlucky nature of ladders. Fast forward hundreds of years, gallows (where people were hung) were often high off the ground and required the soon-to-be-hung person to walk up a ladder. It would be a very ill omen indeed if a bystander were to walk under the same ladder. Today, if you find yourself accidentally strolling underneath a leaning ladder, don't fret, you can cross your fingers while passing through, just don't uncross them until you see a dog! Either that, or spit on your shoe and don't look at it until it has dried—gross but effective.

33. It's bad luck to pass anyone on the staircase

You ascend a flight of stairs, someone else is coming down—what could go wrong? According to an old superstition, you should be wary of crossing paths with someone on a staircase and it could bring bad luck. The origin of this fear might stem from the very real apprehension that you could be pushed off-balance on a staircase! This sounds unreasonable in polite society, but in medieval Europe an assassin or jealous relative could push you down the stairs of a castle and claim that you fell all on your own. Furthermore, wealthy men often carried swords, so a vulnerable person could easily be stabbed in the back while crossing on the stairs. There is a passage in the Bible referring to angels passing each other on a ladder, too, which may add to the superstition. Nowadays, it is more an aspect of etiquette to let the other person finish traversing the step in order to avoid bad luck, but also just in case one of you happens to fall you wouldn't want to bring the other person down with you.

34. Numbers

Certain numbers have folklore behind them ranging from good luck to bad luck, and holiness to bad omens. The number three is seen as important in various religious and cultural texts like the Holy Trinity in Christianity or the division of the sky, seas, and Underworld in Greek mythology. Today, we might say "third time's a charm," "three's a crowd," and "death (or bad things) come in threes." The number three can be taken as good or bad depending on the context and culture.

When it comes to the number nine, it depends on where you are. In the western world, nine is 3x3 (three being an important number in general) and the idiom "that cat has nine lives" is a common phrase. However, in Japan, nine is very unlucky because spoken aloud it sounds a lot like the Japanese word for "suffering" (things aren't priced 9.99 in Japan for a reason).

The number twelve is considered to be a harmonious number because it is easily divisible and many of our historical and cultural building blocks use the number twelve; there are twelve signs of the zodiac, twelve months to a year, twelve gods of Olympus, and twelve tribes of Israel.

Numerous beliefs and superstitions surround the number seven. Often, Christians consider it a holy number, as God took seven days to create the Earth. "Lucky number seven" is synonymous with casino marketing and gambling in the United States. Residents of Rio de Janeiro jump over the ocean waves seven times on New Year's Day for good luck. On the other hand, there are seven deadly sins (really there are eight but the way it is phrased is with seven sins) and breaking a mirror is said to bring seven years of bad luck. Seven is also unique among single-digit numbers as the highest odd number not divisible by any other number. When people are asked to think of a "random" number, seven and seventeen are the most common choices. Perhaps because of their "oddness," they are seen as more random. There are also old wive's tales from different cultures in Eurasia that speak of a "seventh son of a seventh son" having magical powers and a strong destiny for greatness. In Romania, that son is destined to be a vampire, but in Ireland, they are blessed with magical healing powers.

Of all the numbers that have superstitious feelings tied to them, the "unlucky" number thirteen takes the cake. Part of the fear of the number thirteen (known as triskaidekaphobia) stems from Christianity, where Christ held the Last Supper before his crucifixion, and the person who betrayed him, Judas, was supposedly the thirteenth guest. Rumors in the past of a coven of witches having thirteen members and gallows having thirteen steps further increased this superstition.

Not everyone is Christian, of course, so the fear of the number thirteen is mostly prevalent in the western world. In fact, much of Asia has no problem with thirteen while the number "four" sounds like the word for "death" in Chinese-derived languages so they skip using this number in a lot of scenarios. In the United States, the most obvious recognition of triskaidekaphobia is the "missing" thirteenth floor of many skyscrapers. The floors go right from twelve to fourteen, as people would have an instinct to avoid living or working on the thirteenth floor. Whether it's the number on a sports jersey or the number of guests at a party, people in the west have a tendency to avoid the number thirteen whenever possible.

Why was six afraid of seven? Because seven ate nine (reference to the image).

35. A LOAF OF BREAD TURNED UPSIDE DOWN AFTER SLICING IS PERILOUS

Don't turn that loaf of bread upside down, you might invite bad luck! Bread has been a staple food for thousands of years and the Christian faith has symbolism with bread being the "body of Christ." Perhaps that is where the original superstitions around bread came from. But, why is it considered unlucky (especially in France) to slice a piece of bread upside down or even leave it on the table in such a state? The lore stems from the fifteenth century where executioners were a common sight in France as they would travel from city to city performing executions at the King's behest. The King ordered that bakers leave out a loaf of bread for the executioners, who were often busy preparing their blades for the day's beheading. It became customary for bakers to leave a loaf of bread upside down on the counter, signifying that this was the "Executioner's Bread" and all the townspeople knew not to touch it. The superstition evolved, as the upturned bread became synonymous with ill omens and death. If you lay a loaf of bread on its back at the dinner table, you might be inviting the executioner over for dinner!

36. LEFT-HANDED PEOPLE

Roughly one in ten people are left-handed. Unfortunately, people who are different in any way, even if it's just the hand they are more dominant in, have often been the target of superstition and bias throughout history. Even the word "sinister" comes from a Latin word meaning "on the left side." One of the original connotations of the left hand (or left side of the body) being associated with evil was in early Christianity. The Devil sat on God's left side before he was cast out of Heaven and he was normally portrayed as left-handed and left-footed thereafter. Witches, especially in the Middle Ages, were thought to be left-handed. Joan of Arc, who was burned at the stake at nineteen, was even depicted being left-handed, but this was most likely fabricated after the fact. Supposedly, evil spirits lurk over your left shoulder; that is why you should throw salt over your left shoulder to ward them off. If your right ear is ringing, someone is praising you; if your left ear rings, then someone is cursing you. Other things that can be bad luck if you do them with your left hand: passing a drink or pouring a drink, sewing the left sleeve on a dress before the right sleeve, making a toast, or stirring a pot with your left hand could all lead to misfortune.

37. Ouija boards

Ouija boards, otherwise known as spirit boards or talking boards, are often seen in popular culture as a silly game for kids to play or perhaps, on the other extreme, a maligned device to talk to evil spirits.

Movies have a lot to do with the negative reputation of ouija boards, but also the Catholic Church, after a spike in popularity in ouija after World War I, warned that these boards were tantamount to witchcraft and communing with unholy spirits.

The origins of ouija boards are more innocent than we have been led to believe. Speaking to the dead in a ritualistic, group setting (often called a seance) has been around for thousands of years. When two sisters in New York in 1848 began "speaking" to spirits in their home, this evolved to an official religion known as Spiritualism.

In 1897, it was reported by the New York Times that this new religion had eight million followers around the world. Practitioners of Spiritualism started to do "automatic writing" where they claimed a spirit from "Summerland" (their version of the afterlife or spirit world) would direct their hands to write out messages.

This further developed into a wooden board with basic numbers and letters and "yes" or "no" and "hello" or "goodbye" written on it. There was a planchette (a small, heart-shaped object) that was held by someone over the board.

Supposedly, a spirit would be guiding the person's hand across the board and answer questions that the group of believers wanted to know about. The idea was that the spirit world held knowledge and insights that the material world did not have access to.

This grew into a board game that was marketed and sold. It became popular with teenagers as a mild form of rebellion, often done in secret in the basement to avoid adults who might not approve of their kids "speaking" to spirits.

The fear of possession by one of these spirits has been amplified by a combination of religious folks and the media. Of course, Hollywood would use this to market horror movies and play on people's fear of spirits and talking to the dead.

38. It's bad luck to let milk boil over

Before the days of stovetops and ranges, people would heat milk over an open fire. Sometimes, the milk would boil over and spill across the coals, causing bad luck for the house. But don't worry! A prudent person could sprinkle a bit of salt on the coals and keep the good luck intact. Another superstition about milk is that spilling milk will result in seven days of bad luck. Western European lore also added to myths about milk with several superstitions: stepping in a milk bucket would dry up the cows, to make sure a cow was a good milker one should pull a hair from a cow after it is sold, and putting the first milk of a new cow in a bronze bowl made sure that the cow would produce lots of milk in its lifetime. More than likely, these superstitions came about from a desire to not be wasteful with food. In some Indian cultures, spilling milk in a new home actually brings good fortune in the coming years.

39. Placing shoes upon a table will bring bad luck

Putting your feet up on the table, or leaving a shoe on the tabletop, seems like bad manners and unsanitary. But, the superstitions that follow this breach in etiquette are less to do with cleanliness and more about inviting misfortune. The strongest fears about putting shoes on the table say that the person who put them there is inviting bad luck or even death. One possible origin of this involves convicts who were executed by hanging, their shoes would scrape the platform of the gallows, mimicking shoes on a table. The other explanation is more recent, where it was customary to leave the boots of a miner who lost their life on the table out of respect for his hard work and sacrifice. Shoes on the table might mean that a storm is coming, there will be a fight in the household, or, in theater circles, that the upcoming performance is cursed. But is there a remedy if you forget these superstitions and accidentally put your shoes on the table? Yes, supposedly one can knock underneath the table, spit on the soles of the shoes, and the person who placed the shoes on the table must be the one to remove them.

40. Covering the mouth when yawning

In modern society, it is common courtesy to cover your mouth while yawning. This will prevent another person from seeing down your throat and, at least if you're in a conversation, to show the other person that you don't think they're a bore. But this custom, polite as it might be, has an odd origin. Yawning, like sneezing, was once thought to be a gateway to evil spirits or the Devil getting your body. The phrase "God bless you" while sneezing and holding your hand in front of your mouth while yawning stem from this belief that started out with evil spirits and was co-opted by Christianity. Also, there was a belief in some cultures that yawning was an opportunity for the soul to leave the body and that covering your mouth could keep it inside.

41. Never take a broom with you when you move house

Moving into a new home can be stressful and exciting. If you are superstitious, there are certain actions you can take to ensure that your new home is full of love and positive energy. According to the Chinese tradition of feng shui, one should never bring an old broom or mop into a new home. An old broom might have dirt to be sure, but also has swept up all the negative "energy" in the old house. Discard your old one to ensure a fresh beginning. Some people think that the days of the week matter when moving; Thursday is the best day to move while Friday and Saturday are the least lucky. The first guest to your house should bring a gift, cake if possible. Other common superstitions when moving to a new home involve painting the porch blue to ward off evil spirits, having the first item brought into the house be the Bible, hanging a horseshoe over the most commonly used door, and counting the corners of each room for good luck. According to Jewish tradition, bringing bread and salt into the home on the first day you move brings prosperity to the household.

42. Never use a crossroads as a meeting place

Most people use roads and paths on a daily basis. When two roads cross, we think nothing of it. If we look back at history, however, we can see that old cultures viewed a physical crossroads as a setting for a spiritual crossing. Symbolically, a person can decide on two different paths in life at a crossroads and when two forces meet (day and night; good and evil) it can create a conflict or crossroads. In Britain, stones used to be placed at certain crossroads, sometimes as a way to prevent maligned creatures from entering our world. Up until the 1820s, criminals could be buried at crossroads, possibly as a way to confuse their souls or as a warning to others; and "witches," too, would be buried at these intersections. Across medieval European cultures, crossroads were, supposedly, places where vampires, werewolves, banshees, and trolls would congregate. More recently, the blues musician Robert Johnson popularized the dark mythos around crossroads when he recorded "Cross Road Blues" in 1936. In the telling, he sells his soul to the Devil who tunes his guitar and turns him into an amazing musician. This is just a story, but "selling your soul to the Devil" is still in the lexicon today.

43. Palmistry

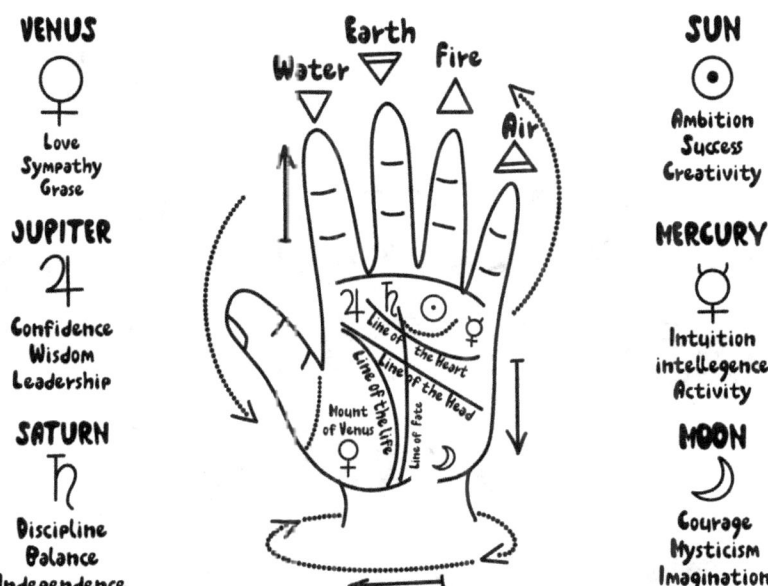

Mystics, seers, diviners, and fortune-tellers have been around since the dawn of civilization. One unique version of foretelling the future involves reading the shape and lines of a person's palms. Palmistry, or chiromancy, has existed for thousands of years and can be seen in the ancient texts of India, Sumeria, China, Greece, and Arabia. It became so popular during the era of witch-hysteria in Europe that a birthmark or other signs on the hand were often given as proof for a witch being in league with the Devil. Serious practitioners of palmistry will see different lines in the hand (Head line, Heart line, Love line, Fate line) and make predictions about the person's future. Overall hand shape and the "mounts" and "plains" of the palm also help the seer to determine one's destiny. Some of the more modern forms of fortune-telling by palm-reading have come from the Roma people of Europe, often called gypsies. Eventually, the Roma were accused of stealing or grifting their customers, but practice has lived on in circuses, carnivals, and back-streets.

44. Pirates

In the modern age, people are obsessed with the stories and legends of pirates. The culture of piracy was brutal and unforgiving, with many unique attributes and traditions that popped up.

Pirates, and quite a few sailors on the high seas, wore earrings. These were often gold and sometimes had their name and hometown engraved on them so if they drowned and washed ashore then they would have the means to be buried from the earring. Another reason was a superstitious belief that earrings protected the wearer from drowning, that if he were to go overboard he would miraculously find his way back to the ship.

Pirates often ate turtles, but to kill one and not eat it was considered very bad luck. Manta rays were feared, as the creatures were thought to attach themselves to anchors and drag ships to the bottom of the ocean.

The rumors that pirates kept exotic animals as pets, like monkeys or parrots, is only partially true. They did keep animals from time to time, but mostly because they would be looking to sell the animal at the next port.

The eyepatch that is commonly seen in media when we think of pirates is not a fabrication, pirates and sailors alike wore eyepatches when they were constantly going back and forth below deck and above deck. The patch allowed one eye to be adjusted to the darkness below deck at all times.

Cats were an integral part of life on many ships, especially on long voyages across the sea. Cats could catch and kill rodents, this prevented the vermin from gnawing on ropes and wood, or from eating the food stores. Cats were believed to be good luck on ships, mostly because of their utility at killing rodents and their companionship. Sailors kept their cats well-fed and happy, as it was considered bad luck if the ship's cat hissed or turned away from a sailor, but it was good luck if the cat came up looking for food or to be scratched.

The stranger superstitions around cats on ships revolves around their tails "controlling" the weather. Some sailors would look at a cat's tail and try to tell if a change in the water was coming. The cats could, supposedly, protect ships from storms but also summon a storm if they fell overboard.

Other cat behavior, like sneezing or excessively licking fur, would often garner scrutiny from the sailors as they were always trying to interpret these actions as omens for the weather. There is some truth to the idea that animals have instincts about changing weather, cats in particular have sensitive inner ears that can sense a change in atmospheric pressure that normally prececes a storm.

45. Vampires

There are countless myths surrounding the nosferatu, Dracula, or any name that a blood-sucking vampire might go by. Vampires are a form of undead and legends about humans who have died and been cursed to walk the earth have been around for untold millenia. Vampires, in particular Dracula, were largely popularized in modern culture by Bram Stoker's 1897 book *Dracula*. Bram Stoker may have partially borrowed from the legend of Vlad the Impaler, a fifteenth century prince in what is now Romania, who was accused of committing gruesome mutilation to his enemies. The superstitions about vampires have largely grown from Stoker's work and the weaving of other lore into the vampire saga. Bram added a fear of garlic to their traditional weakness to sunlight, but garlic has been seen as a medicine for thousands of years, so it seemed natural that those who refused this herb would be seen as suspicious. After the Black Death in Europe, wariness of death and disease led to a fear of "others" and people with aversions to sunlight or garlic were often looked at with apprehension or fear. There is even a medical condition, porphyria, which causes a person's skin to break out into lesions when exposed to too much sunlight that could have contributed to the superstitions about vampires in our midst.

46. Never speak ill of the dead

Since the dawn of humankind, a special reverence and respect has been exhibited for the dead. Showing respect for the people gone from our lives can involve specific cultural burial rites, ceremonies to honor ancestors, or passing down the knowledge that has been bestowed by others. Of course, it is possible to speak badly about those that have passed, but it is often common courtesy in cultures worldwide to "never speak ill of the dead." This phrase can trace back to Chilon of Sparta, one of the Seven Sages of ancient Greece. Supposedly, this philosopher said "don't badmouth a dead man" and the idea and phrase has stuck around for thousands of years. Most of this superstition stems from the belief that the dead go to the afterlife and, if you were to speak ill of them, it could actually harm their experience in the afterlife for all eternity. There is logic to this axiom outside of religious and spiritual settings: most people who are alive wouldn't want to be spoken to unkindly, so why wouldn't the same courtesy apply to the dead? If you were to speak ill of the dead, bad luck might follow you around. Even worse, some rumors say that it will cause the dead spirits to haunt you on earth.

47. Spicy food causes ulcers

If you're hungry and in the mood for something spicy—watch out; there's an old wives' tale that states that spicy food causes stomach ulcers. This was popularized in the 1950s but wasn't proven to any medical extent, it was more the superstitious connection that spicy food can give people a burning sensation in their stomach so it might grow ulcers too. It wasn't until the 1980s when this was shown to be false, as studies showed no connection to the creation of ulcers by spicy food, but that doesn't stop this superstition from sticking around. Another fear about food revolves around chewing gum; specifically, that if you swallow your gum it will stick around in your intestines for seven years! This is completely unfounded, as gum goes through the body just like everything else, but people still pass this belief onto their kids and it keeps sticking around. And why seven years? There seems to be no real reason whatsoever, maybe it is just a good random number. A superstition about the "heat" of the body from eating food stems back to the sixteenth century via the idiom "feed a cold, starve a fever." Some physicians at the time believed that you would want to generate heat in your body by eating food if you had a cold, but that fasting and going without food when you had a fever would bring down your temperature.

48. Scissors

A pair of scissors seems like a silly thing to be superstitious about, but there are plenty of examples in history of people over-reacting to this simple tool. Some cultures believe that when scissors fall and stick into the ground that this is an omen of death. However, some believe that if both points stick into the ground separately, that a wedding will follow. In Egypt, it is bad luck to leave scissors open, or to open them and not cut anything at all. If you drop your scissors you should never pick them up, instead ask someone else to retrieve them for you. If scissors break while in use, then it spells bad luck for the user. Also, superstitious folk will not accept scissors as gifts, for if they do, then the friendship could be severed. An old superstition about scissors comes from the time when Europeans were in constant fear of witches. People would place scissors under their doormats with the blades open, imitating a cross, so that any witches would be prevented from entering the home.

49. Never kill a robin

The phrase "killing two birds with one stone" was definitely not about two robins. In many European cultures, robins represent hope but also danger. The old Celtic traditions have an affinity for robins and they say that if anyone kills the bird then they will bring wrath upon themselves. Perhaps it is the red breast of the robin that symbolizes danger. A robin's song is quite distinct, often it is taken by superstitious folk to mean that rain is looming or that danger is near. Killing a robin in Italy might mean that the perpetrator will suffer from epilepsy. The robin is also associated with storms and can be an omen for death; if a robin taps on your window or flies into your house, it is a sign that a family member will die. If you happen to find a robin's feather, don't hang on to it; carrying it around might mean you are carrying around bad luck wherever you go.

50. Saying bless you when someone sneezes

Everyone sneezes, it is an unavoidable bodily reaction. What could be the harm in a little sneeze? A legend of murky origins states that sneezing is a moment of vulnerability and gives the opportunity for evil spirits to enter your body. Later on, the phrase "bless you" was deemed necessary to be uttered by another person to help keep the evil spirits, or the Devil, from going inside of the sneezing person. This phrase gained prominence during the sixth century when there was a plague besieging Europe. In Rome, Pope Gregory said that sneezing was an early sign of someone getting the plague, so he commanded all loyal Christians to give a blessing, hence "God bless you." In America, due to German immigrants, the German word "Gesundheit" can be interchangeable with "God bless you." This has caught on but it isn't really the same as a blessing, "Gesundheit" simply means "health" in German. Sometimes a sneeze out-of-the-blue can be interpreted by superstitious folks in different ways: a sneeze early in the morning means good fortune will follow later in the day, but if you sneeze on your shoes watch out for misfortune. There is an odd rumor that when you sneeze your heart stops just for a fraction of a second, so saying "bless you" is a way to get it ticking again.

51. THE EVIL EYE

If someone looks at you oddly, could they be giving you a curse? Many people today believe so. There is no universal standard for what the "evil eye" looks like but traditionally it is cast by strangers, childless women, or old women. Often the curse of the evil eye is born out of jealousy and is intended to bring harm on the recipient. Some traditions say that a person can give themselves an evil eye if they act out of greed and without humility. More mildly, in the American lexicon if someone is giving "the evil eye" it simply means a displeased glare; this is contrary to many beliefs in ancient history where it had serious connotations. Greek, Roman, Jewish, Hindu, Muslim, and Buddhist cultures along with many folk religions believe in some form of the evil eye. One way to prevent the curse from sticking to you or to rid yourself of it is to wear an evil eye of your own. These amulets of protection have historical basis, as pendants from ancient Egypt and drinking vessels from ancient Greece have been unearthed with the evil eye adorned on them. In more recent times, the evil eye has been adopted as part of jewelry or decoration, with the intention being that to wear the evil eye (often depicted as a cobalt-blue eye) is to gain protection from others trying to cast the curse.

52. Never bring lilies indoors

Lilies may seem like an innocent flower to bring into your home, but there is folklore and facts that might convince you otherwise. Lilies were initially viewed as symbols of fertility in ancient Greece via a myth about Hera spilling milk on to the Earth that became lilies. Ancient brides wore crowns of lilies with the notion that this would bring fertility to marriage. Lilies became a symbol of Jesus' resurrection and adorn many churches at Easter time. The folklore shifted with the Romans, they would put lilies in the hands of the deceased as a symbol of rebirth. The Catholic church co-opted this practice but eventually the symbolism of death around lilies dominated the superstition. It became unlucky to bring lilies indoors, as it was practically an invitation to bring death into one's home. However, if you own a cat, there is a more practical reason to avoid lilies in your household. The pollen of a lily is poisonous to cats. If they brush against the plant and then lick themselves, they are ingesting a potent toxin, which will pollute and damage the feline's kidneys. Choose another flower to adorn your home—your cat will thank you!

53. Wishbones

Children, especially in America, love to pull apart the dried "wishbone" or furcula of a turkey... seems a bit weird. So where does this odd tradition come from? The Etruscans, of ancient Italy, believed that studying birds could lead to divination (telling the future). They would remove the furcula after slaughtering the animal and leave the bone in the sun to dry. Later, they would stroke the furcula and make a wish, hence "wishbone." This folklore transferred to the Roman Empire, where chickens weren't as common, so villagers would actually crack the bone in half in order to double the number of lucky wishbones. When this practice carried over from Britain to the American Colonies, wild turkeys became the animal of choice for getting a wishbone. A common way to get your wish from a wishbone involves two people pulling the dried, brittle bone apart with their pinky fingers. The person who gets the bigger piece gets their wish! There is no rule that this superstition can't be performed on a daily basis, but it is usually reserved for after the turkey dinner on Thanksgiving in the United States. Furthermore, there is speculation that this is where the expression "lucky break" comes from.

54. BLACK CATS

Everyone agrees that a black cat crossing your path is bad luck, right? Well, hold on, because this isn't a universal belief. This superstition has taken on a second life in modern day America, but in other parts of the world a black cat is nothing to fear. In Scotland, you are lucky if a black cat appears on your doorstep. In some parts of Japan, if you are a single lady and own a black cat, people believe that you will attract a suitor. In Britain, there is a superstition that it is good luck to gift a black cat to a bride on her wedding day; also, British soldiers used to bring black cats on voyages for good luck. The fear of black cats crossing one's path might stem from the Middle Ages, where fear of witches and the Devil was rampant. Cats are nocturnal, solitary, have eyes that glow at night, and aren't as obedient as dogs. These characteristics scared superstitious people, plus their association (right or wrong) with the coming of the Black Plague, probably gave cats their supposed relationship with evil witches. If a black cat crosses your path, the fear is that it is on a mission from a witch (or is a witch itself that has transformed). At the time, the supposed curse could be lifted by going to church and receiving a blessing from the priest.

55. Ravens

Ravens have often been linked with mysticism and the spirit world. This might be due to their nature: ravens are a deep black, have a croaking call, eat carrion (decaying flesh), and travel alone or in pairs. In Greek mythology, Apollo, the God of prophecy, was angered when his raven messenger brought him back news of his lover being unfaithful, so Apollo scorched the raven, turning the once white bird into the black creature we know today. Morrigan (a great warrior-queen goddess in Irish-Celtic mythology) often appeared as a crow or raven when she arrived for battle. Various Native American tribes viewed the raven similar to the coyote, as a trickster and capable of transformation. Raven superstitions have popped up all over the world, including the belief that they bring misfortune or death. Having a raven frequent your house or follow you down a path is considered a very bad omen. However, not all raven folklore is negative. In Norse mythology, Odin is often depicted with two ravens who bring him information and he is often viewed as the god of wisdom. Edgar Allen Poe and Shakespeare, among other writers, have depicted the raven as ominous or evil, perhaps contributing to that belief in popular culture today.

56. THE BLACK DEATH

The Black Death was the first wave of the bubonic plague, a multi-century catastrophe where millions of Europeans were wiped out. In the fourteenth century, rats (more precisely the fleas on them) on trading ships carried the plague to Europe where the bubonic plague spread and whole towns and cities were decimated by the agonizing lesions of this easily transmissible disease. Because the knowledge of medical science was far less sophisticated than in modern times, superstitions abounded about how to deal with the Black Death. The origin of the plague was rumored to have various causes. Some believed it was the wrath of God sent to purge the sinners. A report from the court of the king of France said that the conjunction of the planets in 1345 was the cause as it released "miasmas" (poisonous air). The notion of disease at the time was limited, many physicians believed that diseases were carried from miasmas, instead of by contact with animals or other people. There was an idea that sleeping during the day would spread the plague, and that windows should be left open all the time to release the bad air. There was an instinct to quarantine and avoid the ill, but not to practice hygiene as we know it today; in fact, bathing was often considered almost a vice, or at the very least a temptation, by devoted Christians.

57. Candles

For thousands of years, candles have been a major source of light, but the dancing flames often inspire the imaginations of superstitious folk. Pagan practices of ancient times and large, modern religions across the globe have placed great importance on lighting and using candles in ceremonies. Some ancient Egyptians would stare at a candle before falling asleep in order to ask questions of their gods while they were dreaming. The Celts used candles as a way to keep away evil spirits and would often make sure a lighted candle would stay on the windowsill for protection. This tradition would live on, as many religious ceremonies consider the flame "holy;" and, in modern pop culture and scary movies, if all the candles suddenly blow out in a room, there is often a malevolent force lurking nearby. In other parts of Europe, a candle in the window was said to draw spirits, and if the candle started to blow then the spirit had arrived. Even the collection of wax around the wick could be interpreted as a death in the family being imminent. A very common belief was that if a candle refused to light, then a storm was coming.

58. Owls

Owls have traditionally been seen as supernatural birds; constantly hooting in the night, silent predators with bright eyes, able to turn their heads completely around. As far back as Greek mythology, where the goddess Athena had a little owl as a companion, owls have been seen as foreboding creatures. The Romans believed that owls foretold the death of emperors, and that nailing an owl to a door would prevent evil spirits from entering. This practice continued in the eighteenth century in Britain, with farmers nailing owls to barn doors to protect their livestock. Both the Greeks and Romans thought that witches could turn into owls and later, in medieval cultures, an owl's hooting was considered a warning that witches were approaching. Some believed that owls were the only animals that could live beside ghosts, so an owl alone in an abandoned building was a very bad omen indeed. However, not all cultures worldwide thought of the owl as a spooky animal. The Aborigines of Australia protected owls as they were considered to hold the spirits of women. The Kwakiutl people of Canada thought that the souls of the deceased became owls, therefore killing an owl was taboo as the soul of that person in the owl would be killed as well.

59. Bigfoot

Does Bigfoot exist? Tales of giant, hairy, bipedal creatures living in the mountains or forests have existed for centuries. Whether they go by Bigfoot or sasquatch, there have been too many "sightings" throughout history to ignore the possibility of their existence. The people of the Himalayan mountains have folklore about a similar creature to Bigfoot called a yeti, mostly with white fur as the main difference, though different color patterns have been told in folk tales.

The legend of Bigfoot in the western hemisphere has origins in indigenous tribes of Canada and the United States, with stories about entire families of large, hairy creatures. The myths evolved and any variation of sasquatch is almost guaranteed to be viewed as a solitary being in popular culture today.

Some stories have Bigfoot knocking on trees as it wanders the forest, other tales tell of it stealing from encampments or attacking settlers. Most believers in the legend admit that the creature is excellent at hiding and prefers solitude above all else.

The sheer number of stories from early settlers in America and Native

American stories passed down from generations kept the legend alive into the twentieth century. Then, in California, an infamous video was recorded in 1958 that showed a "creature" that looked like Bigfoot walking through a forest clearing.

Hoopla and questions surrounded the authenticity of the video, but the legend of Bigfoot only continued to grow from that point on. In modern times, there have been over 10,000 reported Bigfoot sightings! Many are in the Pacific northwest region of America but the range of sightings extends from northern Canada to the southeastern United States.

There have been television shows, books, and many long weekends spent searching for the mysterious Bigfoot. Is there archeological evidence for a larger-than-man creature that walks on two legs? Well, bears, which are common in the United States and Canada, can stand on two legs. Perhaps it is a case of mistaken identity. Our species, homo sapiens, is just one of many evolutionary off-shoots; some of our ancestors were much shorter than the average person is today. Who knows if perhaps there was a larger, hairy, primal version of humankind that has been lost to the great wilderness...

60. Burning cheeks mean someone is talking about you

We've all had moments in our lives where our cheeks are warm and flushed, perhaps our ears get red too or our stomachs flutter. But what does it mean? Often, our own anxious thoughts or sense of embarrassment can trigger such a reaction, but what if it comes out of the blue? Some superstitions claim that burning cheeks means that someone is thinking or talking about you, whether that is in the same vicinity or at a distance. If your cheeks get flushed then someone might be disrespecting or talking bad about you, almost like they physically "slapped" you. In Russian lore, if your right cheek is burning then it is a good omen and someone close to you is thinking about you; however, if your left cheek is red then an enemy is spreading gossip and lies against you. In some variations, getting red in the ears means that someone who likes you is talking about you. Take note of the first person who comes to mind after you become flushed, it might just be who is speaking about you.

61. Picking up pennies

Sometimes the opportunity to increase your luck might be lying on the street. An old wives' tale is summarized in a rhyme: "Find a penny, pick it up, all the day you'll have good luck." This superstition originated in ancient times when many cultures used heavy metals to make coins and some people believed that these metals could offer protection against evil spirits. To see a random coin on the ground was considered a gift from the gods. Logically, picking up a coin also increases your wealth, even if a penny isn't worth much nowadays. For the very superstitious among us, they only pick up a penny and keep it if it is lying heads up on the ground; the good news is that they might flip over a tails up penny to leave for the next passerby. Some people believe that the best way to ensure good luck is to pass the penny on to a different person. A lucky penny can also be used by a bride on her wedding day, as the old phrase tells us: "Something old, something new, something borrowed, something blue and a penny in the shoe." The penny (or sixpence as the original rhyme goes) was supposed to bring love and happiness to the newlyweds.

62. Keeping cats away from babies

This superstition sounds odd—and terrifying. Millions of households across the world have cats, why would they be perceived as a threat to a baby? There existed some rumors about cats being attracted to the scent of milk on a baby's breath or feeling jealous of the attention of a newborn, but the obscene fear of a cat literally sucking a child's breath away is almost entirely based on a single report from 1791. In the publication "Annual Register," there is an article which reads: "A child of eighteen months old was found dead near Plymouth; and it appeared, on the coroner's inquest, that the child died in consequence of a cat sucking its breath, thereby occasioning a strangulation." This story took on a life of its own, and added to previous lore that cats have long been believed to be companions of witches. Cats have been seen in both positive and negative lights for thousands of years, with the Egyptians worshiping them, and some distant fear of cats appearing in Hebrew mythology, as the dark goddess Lilith could change into a vampire cat and then suck the blood of newborn infants.

63. Ships as "she"

Captains and sailors have referred to their ships as feminine for thousands of years. Though not a universal practice, it is interesting that so many cultures have deferred to this method of identification. Most people consider an unnamed ship unlucky, but sometimes the names can be places instead of people or deities, so why not just call the ship "it" instead of "she"? Part of the reason might be language itself, many Latin languages have genders for words, and the Latin word for ship is feminine (navis). Another name for a ship is a vessel, and things like pottery or vases were often considered feminine, as they are meant to protect things similar to a womb. Sailors are superstitious and, historically, have been predominantly male. Having a ship that "protects" them from the ocean is like a mother protecting her child. In ancient times, sailors looked to goddesses to help them in their journeys; indeed, some of the first figureheads carved into the front of large, sea-faring vessels were female goddesses. Also, a ship was like a partner to the sailors, something they loved and cared for, so in that regard they would view it as a female companion.

64. The first person you see on new year's day must be a dark haired man

This superstition is as weird and specific as any other. Wanting to know who it is that enters your home is normal. It is this general anxiety paired with the importance of ringing in a new year that gives this superstition its foundation. The ancient Greeks may have had a similar story of the first person to enter bringing either good or bad luck, but the modern version is derived from Scottish and Northern English lore. Often referred to as "first-footing," this is a practice where the first person to enter a home after the new year was important in determining the luck of the household for the entire year. The man (sometimes referred to as the "Lucky Bird") should be tall, dark-haired, handsome and, if possible, be bearing a small gift for the household. Sometimes this gift would be silver, salt, a sprig of evergreen, or coal. The idea of a "dark-haired man" might come from the Viking invasion of the British Isles, where blonde-haired men (the Vikings) were seen as a threat to the English countryside. It was even encouraged to have a guest that fit the description (or even the homeowner themself) slip out of the house before the stroke of midnight just so they could be the first person to enter the house.

65. KNOCK ON WOOD

Touching or knocking on wood has been a cure-all for curses and bad luck, or as a simple demonstration that you hope some outcome will occur. It is often used to temper a boast you've made; if you made a bold promise or claim, you might knock on wood as "insurance" that your outcome will occur in a favorable manner. In western cultures, this superstition is as common as saying "bless you" when someone sneezes. The origin has to do with the pagan belief that guiding spirits lived in trees. By knocking on the wood you were acknowledging the spirit and it would return the favor by granting you a good outcome or preventing an ill fate. Another possible avenue for touching wood to become popularized was a form of tag from Britain from the nineteenth century where players couldn't be tagged if they were touching wood. Later, as with many superstitions, Christians put a spin on the old wives' tale and knocking on wood became symbolic to touching Jesus' cross, thereby getting close to his divine power. Most people aren't living in the forest, so touching or knocking on any piece of wood can suffice. Nowadays, there isn't always real wood in our plastic-dominated world, so some people have taken to merely saying the phrase "knock on wood" to give themselves a measure of luck.

66. Seeing a shooting star

When we see a streak of light in the sky we call it a "shooting star." Essentially, when meteors (small space particles) enter Earth's atmosphere they are falling at extreme velocity and it creates intense friction with the gasses in the atmosphere, giving a fiery appearance. For millennia, humans have conjured up superstitions about shooting stars. Sailors believed that the direction a shooting star takes across the sky will determine which way the wind will blow. Various cultures have claimed that shooting stars are souls released from purgatory and that they are traveling up to heaven. In Great Britain, it is said that a shooting star represents the soul of a newborn baby coming to Earth. If you see a falling star and say "money, money, money" then you will come into wealth in the near future. If you happen to spot a shooting star on the start of a trip then your voyage will be a fortunate one. Most agree that shooting stars are good luck, though if you see one on your left then it might be unlucky. But if you are quick and switch your stance, then you can reverse your fortune if it falls on your right side.

67. Spilling salt

You reach for the mashed potatoes and knock over the salt shaker, everyone glares at you, but it's just a little salt, right? According to a persistent superstition, spilling salt is very bad luck. This belief stems from centuries ago when salt was a valuable commodity, it was a common basis for exchange among trading partners. Spilling salt would be seen as wasting it and throwing away money. There is even a rumor, one that has no solid historical basis but has persisted nonetheless, that the Romans used salt as currency. The world 'salary' is actually derived from the Latin word for salt. Further superstitions emerged, one stating that if you spill salt towards someone then you are sending them a curse. In Leonardo da Vinci's painting *The Last Supper*, Judas is depicted as having spilled salt, further pushing this legend into the popular consciousness. Salt has been used by various cultures to ward off evil spirits and bless new homes. The best way to counteract the bad luck from spilling salt is to throw a pinch over your left shoulder. This may sound counter-intuitive, after all, aren't you wasting more salt? But the superstition has shifted to simply being reactive and preventing ill luck from following you. By throwing salt over your left shoulder you are throwing it in the direction of the Devil, as he is said to be lurking on your left side.

68. Carrying a Toadstone to Protect Against Evil and Cure Illness

In the ancient world, fossils were often mistaken for stones. The uniqueness of some fossils led people to speculate that they had magical powers. Toadstones were thought to come from the head of a toad, but in reality they are the fossilized teeth of the long-extinct Lepidotes fish. They were often smooth and round and could be quite valuable as in parts of Europe they would sit beside a necklace or ring of a noble. The use of toadstones was recorded nearly two thousand years ago by Roman author Pliny the Elder and continued in Europe until the eighteenth century. People would wear them as talismans or carry them in their pockets. They were said to ward off evil and bring good luck. One of the main superstitions was that toadstones could protect against poison. Supposedly, the stones could change color and heat up in the presence of poison. Some folks would place a toadstone on bites from snakes or spiders in order to extract the venom. Also, swallowing the stone would help cleanse the body and counteract poisons.

69. Tying a Knot in a Handkerchief

Have you ever lost something and scratched your head trying to remember where you left it? You are not alone and, thankfully, there is an old remedy to your problem. A superstitious person might suggest that you tie a knot in a handkerchief, rope, or string and soon enough you will remember where your lost item is located. Sometimes you need to rub the knot to jog your memory. This superstition might have its roots in the Greek myth of the Minotaur's labyrinth, where the princess Ariadne gave Theseus a thread to find his way out of the labyrinth. In the coming centuries, with the advent of Christianity, the rumor that the Devil or some other demon caused forgetfulness was widely believed, so tying a knot was a way to secure your memory from the Devil. Soldiers in World War I tied handkerchiefs into knots as a way to pray for the end of the war. Whether or not these superstitions are true, there is some logic to tying knots to find lost things. It is a bit of a trick of human psychology, as the act of tying the knot could help you focus and give you confidence in your quest to find what you lost.

70. Gravestones

The original iteration of gravestones, otherwise known as tombstones or grave markers, is a bit spooky. In more primitive times, large stones or boulders were placed over the graves of the recently deceased in order to prevent them from rising up and terrorizing the living. This superstition later changed to stone slabs placed at the head of the grave to mark the burial site and often included an inscription of the person who was laid to rest. Other superstitions arose around burials and gravestones. Some Christian traditions say that graves should be dug so that the head is laid towards the west, so that the dead won't need to turn around when Gabriel blows his trumpet during revelation. The reverse is sometimes invoked, as laying the dead person's head pointing east would be the direction of the star that shone at Jesus' birth. Supposedly, the shovels and any tools used to dig the grave should never be brought home that day, but rather picked up the following day to prevent bad luck. Also, graves should never be left open overnight, as it invites another death to follow. Digging and filling the grave on the same day is paramount.

71. Crossed knives at the table signify a quarrel

When eating with friends and family, table etiquette should be observed. But does it matter if you are a little sloppy and two of your silverware cross each other? According to superstitious folks, the answer is yes! Crossing knives at the dinner table means that a quarrel is imminent. The person who did the crossing must straighten the knives immediately in order to avoid conflict. In the past, crossing a knife with a fork meant that the person was a practitioner of witchcraft. Sometimes, if a knife was crossed with a spoon, it meant that you didn't like the chef's cooking. Knives often have symbolism attached to them. For instance, if you gift a knife to a friend, it might mean that the friendship will soon be severed, but if they give you just a penny as payment for the gift, then everything will be alright. A weird superstition says that placing a knife under the bed of a woman giving birth will ease her pain. Also, some people believe you should never stir anything with a knife as this will bring bad luck. There is a rhyme to help you remember this rule: stir with a knife and stir up strife.

72. Always stir Christmas pudding clockwise

A fun Christmas tradition, historically performed in western European households, is the making of a Christmas pudding. Originally called "plum" pudding, this holiday dish has many superstitions regarding its preparation. Traditionally, Christmas pudding is made on the Sunday before Christmas, known as "Stir-up Sunday," which allows time for the pudding to settle and for God's blessing to be imparted on all who helped make it. Thirteen ingredients should be used, representing Jesus and his twelve disciples, and every member of the family should help stir it—but only clockwise! This is to mimic the east to west journey of the Three Wise Men in the Bible. A counterclockwise stir would be synonymous with the Devil. A garnish of holly might be placed on top to represent the crown of thorns worn by Jesus. In England, silver coins would be placed inside the pudding for good fortune in the year to come. This probably stems from the times when peas or beans were placed inside the pudding. Other lucky charms that might be added inside would be a ring (for a potential marriage), a thimble (for thrift and fortune), or a wishbone (for luck).

73. Frogs

Frogs have carried strong symbolism and superstition for centuries. In ancient Egypt, Hekt was the frog-headed goddess that represented birth and fertility. The Egyptians believed that if you wanted to have a child then you should touch a frog for luck. This connection makes a certain amount of sense, as frogs would come out in the millions after the Nile River flooded yearly, and this flooding (and croaking) would signify a bountiful season. In Britain, there is an old legend that says carrying a dried frog in a pouch would prevent epilepsy. In parts of Appalachia in the United States, it is thought that if you hear a frog croaking at midnight then rain is on the way. In other cultures, if a frog is croaking during the day then a storm is coming. In Ireland, some superstitious folk believe that you can tell the weather by the color of a frog. The Xhosa people of Africa have lore that says a frog in the house might be carrying a curse, but other cultures think it is good luck for a frog to enter the home.

74. Covering mirrors after a death in the home

Mirrors, or reflective surfaces in general, have often been associated with the spirit world. This idea traces back to ancient Greece and Rome where mystics looked into pools of water to tell the future or speak to the dead. Mirrors as "soul portals," where dead spirits could linger, only grew during the centuries. The strongest tradition about covering mirrors after a death comes from Judaism. After a person in the family dies, the Jewish tradition states that a sitting shiva (a week-long mourning period) should be performed. All reflective surfaces in the house must be covered, this encourages the living members to mourn and reflect without practicing vanity. Variations of this superstition persist across the globe. In Victorian England, before a funeral, all the clocks would be stopped and the mirrors would be covered to prevent the dead person's soul from being trapped on Earth. In the Russian Orthodox church, the mirrors are covered with black cloth to help the deceased's journey to the afterlife. Buddhists in Sri Lanka turn over or cover any reflective surfaces so that the soul of the deceased doesn't get confused and can safely make its way to the afterlife.

75. Magpies

Magpies are clever birds; so smart, in fact, that they can recognize themselves in a mirror! Perhaps people in ancient times created superstitions around these birds because they could see the intelligence they displayed. A famous nursery rhyme tells us what it means if we come across a single magpie or a flock of the birds:

> One for sorrow, two for joy,
> Three for a girl, four for a boy,
> Five for silver, six for gold,
> Seven for a secret never to be told.

As far back as ancient Greece, magpies have been recognized as ominous birds, with the Greeks even studying their behavior (called "ornithomancy") in order to read omens of the future. In Germany and Scandinavia, magpies were associated with witches and malevolent spirits. The superstitions about bad luck from magpies is still alive in Great Britain and Ireland today, with some wary folk going so far as to greet and converse with a solitary magpie in the hopes of warding off ill omens.

76. FULL MOON

When the moon is full, strange things happen; at least, that is the superstition. Many ancient cultures worshiped the moon or attributed other-worldly powers to it. Even the "father of modern medicine," the Greek physician Hippocrates, thought insanity was caused by the moon goddess, Luna, riding her chariot across the night sky. This is a derivative of where we get the word "lunacy" from.

Some Chinese folk religions made offerings to their ancestors during full moons and several Native American tribes told legends about the full moon's influence. In popular culture, werewolves are thought to be active on full moons. An urban legend states that people are more violent and aggressive on full moons.

Nocturnal animals might also be more active on a full moon, but there is some logic to all this energetic behavior: a full moon means that there is more light to see. Being able to see better in the dark means more night time activities. This could, theoretically, be a reason for humans causing trouble on a moonlit night.

Some people attribute bad luck to a full moon on a Sunday and good luck if one falls on a Monday ("Moon day"). The moon goes through phases and odd superstitions have spread about the phases of the moon controlling women's menstrual cycles. This is only a coincidence as each cycle is, on average, twenty-eight days.

Some people might think that full moons make a pregnant woman go into labor, but nothing in the statistical evidence bears this out. Modern rumors about not scheduling any surgery during a full moon have sprung up as well. Some people surmise that if the moon affects the ocean's tides then it might shift a person's blood, but this isn't backed up by science whatsoever.

There are even superstitions regarding moonlight itself. Drawing the curtains on a moonlit night was considered prudent in the medieval world, as sleeping in moonlight was thought to cause insomnia and headaches.

Up until the mid-twentieth century, it was rumored that hanging a baby's nappy (diaper) out at night in the moonlight was bad luck. There is a relatively benign superstition about the first light of a new moon: that if you see a sliver of moonlight through the window you will break a dish.

77. Bats want to nest in women's hair

In popular culture, we often view bats as scary creatures that fly at night, with the added fear that they might suck your blood! However, only three out of 1,200 bat species actually "drink" blood and bats are afraid of humans (we are, after all, much larger). In some mythologies, notably Chinese and Persian, bats are symbols of happiness and longevity. The link to bats and evil is rooted in the imagery of the Devil with bat wings in paintings from the Middle Ages. Christians in Europe saw nocturnal creatures like bats as synonymous with evil doings. But, the fear of bats getting tangled into a woman's long hair took on a life of its own. Superstitions that the bat was trying to nest in the hair arose, with a range of specific fears: that the bats would steal hair and bring it back to witches for a potion, the bats would cause baldness, or they would give one a headache and lice. An old French wives' tale says that a bat in the hair means that a disastrous love affair is coming. There is little evidence that bats actually want to get tangled in anyone's hair. Bats hunt small insects, so it wouldn't be abnormal for a bat to swoop near a person, as they might see a small meal nearby.

78. Loose or broken shoelaces

If your shoelace comes untied while you're walking, wouldn't it be safe and smart to tie it? Yet, an odd superstition states that you should walk another nine paces before tying your shoe, or else bad luck will follow you for the rest of the day. Shoelaces are a comparatively recent invention, straps and leather bands were used for ancient footwear, but the fear that a shoe will break or come undone is something any generation can relate to. The Romans perceived a broken shoe strap as bad luck; it was even rumored that the Emperor Augustus had one break when he was running for his life during an assassination attempt. A broken shoelace is bad luck, but an untied shoelace can be an ambivalent message. An old wives' tale says that if your left shoelace comes undone then someone is bad-mouthing you, whereas if your right shoelace comes loose someone is speaking highly of you. A more romantic superstition from England says that if your shoelace came undone accidentally, this meant that your true love was thinking of you. An odd superstition has newlyweds hang their shoes by their laces on the back of their car as they drive away in order to give themselves good luck after their wedding.

79. BRINGING A HAWTHORN BRANCH INTO THE HOUSE WILL BRING DEATH

Hawthorn trees grow easily across the northern hemisphere and many superstitions have arisen around this plant, especially on the British Isles. However, one of the first magical legends around the hawthorne was from ancient Greece where the wood of a hawthorn tree was used as a torch on a couple's wedding night. The most alarming myth from Britain says that if you cut a hawthorn branch and bring it, or its flowers, into the house then it will bring death to your mother. This fear could have come about because Jesus' crown of thorns may have been hawthorn. Also, the hawthorn tree was associated with pagan beliefs about witches and fairies. Witches supposedly made their brooms from hawthorn branches. Fairies may have used hawthorn trees, especially those trees standing alone in the wild, as portals to enter humanity's realm. This superstition was reinforced as farmers in Britain used hawthorn trees extensively as boundaries around their property starting in the eighteenth century. Lone hawthorn trees were especially dangerous on mystical holidays like May Day, midsummer, or Hallowen. Ironically, another superstition states that May Day is the only day where hawthorn can safely be brought into a home, as this was the day that the plant traditionally blossomed.

80. Holding your breath when passing a cemetery

Cemeteries have inspired fears and superstitions for generations. Visiting a graveyard at night is taboo, as is desecrating the headstones or burial mounds of the dead. A common folk tale, especially prevalent in America, says that you must hold your breath when driving past a cemetery or the spirits might be jealous of your breath and haunt you. The origin of this superstition is unknown, but it is nearly always associated with driving so it must be recent in history. This fear could be downstream from the connection between life and breath that many ancient cultures believed. Some people thought that breathing, or especially sneezing or yawning, were vulnerable openings for evil spirits to enter a body. In another telling, if you breathe while going past a cemetery you will breathe in the spirit of a recently deceased person and they could possess your body. Other superstitions about cemeteries include: it is bad luck to point at a grave (the dead will see you), never whistle inside the walls of a cemetery (you might summon the Devil), and don't be the first to leave the cemetery after a funeral (it is bad luck and could bring death to you).

81. Acorns protect your house from lightning

To protect your home from a thunderstorm, on your windowsill you should place... an acorn? This may seem like a silly superstition but it was quite common up until the mid-twentieth century in northern Europe and England. Oak trees were associated with Thor, the Norse god of thunder. They were said to be safe during a lightning storm, and if an oak branch or just an acorn was kept in the home then the house wouldn't be struck by lightning. More recently, some superstitious pilots have taken acorns in their flight suits. The bottoms of blind-cords were occasionally fashioned to look like acorns. Another superstition states that mirrors should be covered during a storm to prevent them from attracting lightning. Thunder and lightning have always fascinated the imagination, we might even assume that prehistoric mankind saw the fire that lightning made as a divine gift. It has made its way into popular lore, like Santa Claus naming his reindeer Donner and Blitzen after the German words for thunder and lightning. There is the modern day saying that "lightning never strikes the same place twice," but this doesn't have scientific basis. In fact, tall buildings especially have been recorded to have dozens or hundreds of lightning strikes at the same place.

82. Breaking a mirror

Smash! The fear that a broken mirror will bring bad luck is prevalent in cultures worldwide, from China to India to Europe to America. The specific fear that this bad luck will follow you around for seven years has become mainstream in popular culture. The ancient Greeks believed that spirits lived in pools of water. The Romans added to the myth the seven year part, they believed that a person's "life cycle" would renew every seven years. This morphed into a broken mirror causing one's soul to break and misfortune to follow until the seven year life cycle is up. Other beliefs blossomed from these ideas, like the damaged soul in the mirror would seek revenge against the person who broke the glass. A multitude of remedies for the curse have been proposed across cultures. If you bury the shattered pieces by the light of the moon or if you use the biggest piece to reflect the moonlight, you can get rid of the bad luck. Other solutions include grinding all of the pieces into dust and scattering them in the wind. Or, you can take a fragment and touch it against a gravestone and bury the rest. Lastly, throwing all of the pieces into a flowing river might do the trick. The key seems to be not to just sweep the broken mirror into the trash, you have to do some ritual of respect to reverse the curse.

83. Pregnancy

Pregnancy is an important and stressful time for a mom-to-be; it makes sense that superstitions have flourished about how to have a healthy, happy pregnancy. Many of these old wives' tales vary depending on the country and culture that one is raised in.

In China, attending a wedding while pregnant is frowned upon because of the clash of "qi" energy or luck. Having two joyous things happening at once (a pregnancy and a wedding) might sound fantastic, but in Chinese culture they consider this a clash of harmony and these significant life events might compete with each other and bring misfortune to the unborn child. The Chinese also have a superstition that rubbing your belly while pregnant, which seems nearly unavoidable, should be steered clear of because it will lead to the child being spoiled and demanding as a baby.

A widespread belief in Polynesia and Hawaii says that leis shouldn't be worn while pregnant. The fear is that the loop of the lei can cause the umbilical cord to strangle the baby inside of the mother.

In India, eclipses are looked at as auspicious events for anyone who is pregnant. The mother is advised to rest, cover the windows, avoid using sharp objects, and not bathe until the eclipse has passed.

Anyone who has ever been pregnant knows one thing for sure: you need to eat for two. An increased appetite is normal and there is often specific food one might crave. In various cultures, there is an idea that a pregnant person should eat whatever they are craving because if they avoid a particular food then the baby will have a birthmark in the shape of that food.

This may seem silly, but it has enough tradition behind it that the word birthmark translates to "craving" in multiple languages. The possible real-world connection is that eating enough food overall is important for the development of a healthy baby, but the birthmark myth has no basis in modern science whatsoever.

Avoiding funerals and cemeteries when pregnant is a strong superstition for Orthodox Jews and is present in some Native American tribes as well, as they say it is dangerous for the mother to be so close to death as recently departed souls linger around cemeteries.

The Hmong people (ethnic group from Southeast Asia) believe that a pregnant person should avoid large bodies of water, as evil spirits may try to steal the unborn baby if the mother enters the water.

84. Nessie

The Loch Ness monster, or Nessie as it is commonly referred, is a creature that supposedly lurks in the depths of Loch Ness in Scotland. Sighted by many, but disputed by most zoologists, this dinosaur-like monster has inspired people to plumb the depths of Loch Ness, searching for its elusive presence. Much of the hype around Nessie is due to a murky photograph taken in 1934 that "shows" Nessie's long neck above the waters of the lake. Tourists and debates have swirled since that time. Explanations vary as to the true nature of Nessie sightings, is it a case of mistaken identity with other animals, or just the human imagination run amok? The references to creatures in Scottish lochs has a basis in folklore. "Kelpies" were magical creatures, originally described as water-horses, that were said to inhabit lochs, and even Loch Ness is pointed to as having a long history with these mythical creatures. As time went on, and evidence was discovered of dinosaurs like the ocean-dwelling plesiosaurus that Nessie might resemble, people began to "see" the longer-necked Nessie as opposed to a water-horse. Whether it is Bigfoot, Nessie, or the yeti, mysterious and hard-to-find creatures are persistent in the myths of our natural world.

85. Voodoo dolls

Voodoo, or Vodou, is a religion predominantly found in the Caribbean. Contrary to popular concepts, Voodoo dolls are not malicious effigies meant to curse people. The Voodoo dolls used by serious practitioners are meant to heal and communicate with the deceased. The dolls sold to tourists and popularized by movies and media are often made to resemble an enemy. Sometimes a lock of the enemy's hair is stolen and put on the doll and pins are pushed into the doll to cause spiritual and physical harm to that person. Typical Voodoo dolls that one might see for sale aren't the real religious effigies. To harm another person isn't the purpose of Voodoo dolls at all, as the pins that practitioners of Voodoo stick into their dolls are meant to release negative energy and help bring about other fortuitous outcomes. The color of these cloth dolls often serves a purpose, whether it is to aid in healing or bring about love and new relationships. This practice probably stems from West Africa and came to the Americas via the slave trade. A new mixture of European, African, and New World cultures blended together and one result was the Voodoo religion and the Creole language.

86. Never light three cigarettes with one match

Superstitions don't have to be old beliefs that have been passed down for millenia, sometimes they are based on modern events. During World War I, a superstition arose that said if three soldiers lit their cigarettes with one match, then one of them would die. There was a logic for the soldiers in this fear: an enemy sniper might see the match being lit and look in the direction of the flame as the first soldier lit his cigarette. The sniper would then aim as the second man took the match, then fire and kill the third soldier as he lit his cigarette. This took on a serious meaning for the soldiers and they brought it back home after leaving the frontlines of Europe; most notably, the American soldiers returning from war in 1918 spread the belief that "three to a match" was very bad luck. Another reason relates to the number "three" itself, as many Christians view this number as sacred because of the Holy Trinity. They would avoid doing a disrespectful or casual act "in threes." Lighting a flame had a connection to hell and the Devil, so having three cigarettes with one match could be seen as disrespecting the Holy Trinity. This may have combined with the soldiers' fear of snipers from World War I to form the contemporary superstition that "three to a match" is bad luck and invites misfortune.

87. Water

Water is the most essential element for every human's survival. It makes sense that superstitions about water would pop up in cultures all over the world. A common superstition says that if someone is leaving on a journey, you should spill water behind them as they leave and this will bring them good luck. In Wales, if a woman splashes water around when she washes clothes then she will be cursed with a drunken husband. In Nigeria, it is taboo among the Yoruba people to fetch from a well at night, as an evil spirit may slap you in the dark. This might be practical advice rooted in reality, as predators could be lurking near the well at night. The Germans have an odd superstition, stemming from Greek mythology, that you should never make a toast with water. If you do, you are wishing death upon the people you are drinking with! Another odd tradition from Yorkshire, England, involves pouring hot water on the threshold of a church after a wedding ceremony. This would keep the doorstep warm as a blessing for the next couple to be married.

88. Lady luck

Who is "Lady Luck"? Is there a mysterious force, a muse, or a mystical energy that gives away luck to those wise enough to see or feel this lady of luck? Frank Sinatra's song "Luck Be a Lady" talks about Lady Luck like she is a real person and helped to bring this superstition into popular culture. Often, Lady Luck is more of an personification of luck itself, that if you are doing poorly then "something" needs to come along and give you good luck. Lady Luck might be said to be following you around if you are having a great day full of fortune and happiness. There are shockingly few references to Lady Luck in history. The Greek goddess Tyche, later named Fortuna by the Romans, might be the closest representation to Lady Luck that we have. She is the goddess of fortune and luck (both good and bad luck) and is usually depicted as blind and veiled, much like the "Lady Justice" statues that adorn many judicial buildings across the western world. The Virgin Mary may also have a role as Lady Luck for Christians later on, as praying to her was a way to pray for good fortune.

Bonus

Thanks for supporting me and purchasing this book! I'd like to send you some freebies. They include:

- The digital version of *500 World War I & II Facts*
- The digital version of *101 Idioms and Phrases*
- The audiobook for my best seller *1144 Random Facts*

Scan the QR code below, enter your email, and I'll send you all the files. Happy reading!

Thank you to my amazing illustrators!

Zhanna

Paul

www.ingramcontent.com/pod-product-compliance
Lightning Source LLC
Chambersburg PA
CBHW072102110526
44590CB00018B/3277